Command Kung Fu

JASON CANNON

JASON CANNON

ISBN: 1499222033
ISBN-13: 978-1499222036

CONTENTS

YOUR FREE GIFT

As a thank you for reading *Command Line Kung Fu*, I would like to give you a copy of *Linux Alternatives to Windows Applications*. In it, you will be introduced to over 50 of the most popular applications available for Linux today. These applications will allow you to browse the web, watch movies, listen to music, connect to your favorite social networks, create presentations, and more. This gift is a perfect complement to this book and will help you along your Linux journey. Visit http://www.linuxtrainingacademy.com/linux-apps to download your free gift.

JASON CANNON

INTRODUCTION

I have been working at the command line on Unix and Linux systems since the 1990's. Needless to say, I feel right at home with nothing more than a dollar sign and a flashing cursor staring at me. Over the years I've picked up several command line "tricks" that have saved me time and frustration.

Some of these tips were born out of necessity — I simply had too much work to complete and too little time to do it in. Others were modeled after popular patterns found in computer programming and application development. The rest were shared with me, either directly or indirectly, by my command line heroes and mentors. It's amazing what you can learn by watching, emulating, and taking advice from a seasoned Unix and Linux professional.

Even though the title is *Command Line Kung Fu*, you don't have to be a Linux ninja to use the tactics presented in this book. The tips work as presented. You can start putting them to use immediately without fully understanding all the details and nuances. However, if you want or need more information, explanations and practical real-world examples follow each one.

Also, if you want to see some of these commands in action visit http://www.linuxtrainingacademy.com/fu. There you will find a series of videos that demonstrate some of the commands covered in this book.

Finally, if you want an overview of the Linux command line and operating system please read my other book *Linux for Beginners*. It will give you a strong foundation upon which you can build your Linux skills.

Let's get started.

SHELL HISTORY

Run the Last Command as Root

```
$ sudo !!
$ su -c "!!"
```

If you ever forget to run a command with root privileges, you can simply repeat it by using sudo !! or su -c "!!".

```
$ adduser sam
-bash: /usr/sbin/adduser: Permission denied
$ sudo !!
sudo adduser sam
$ id sam
uid=1007(sam) gid=1007(sam) groups=1007(sam)
$ userdel -r sam
-bash: /usr/sbin/userdel: Permission denied
$ sudo !!
```

```
sudo userdel -r sam
$ id sam
id: sam: No such user
$ useradd jim
-bash: /usr/sbin/useradd: Permission denied
$ su -c "!!"
su -c "useradd jim"
Password:
$ id jim
uid=1007(jim) gid=1007(jim) groups=1007(jim)
```

This exclamation mark syntax is called an event designator. An event designator references a command in your shell history. Bang-Bang (!!) repeats the most recent command, but one of my favorite uses of the event designator is to run the most recent command that starts with a given string. Here's an example.

```
$ whoami
jason
$ uptime
12:33:15 up 35 min, 1 user, load average: 0.00, 0.00,
0.00
$ df -hT /boot
Filesystem Type Size Used Avail Use% Mounted on
/dev/vda1 ext4 485M 55M 406M 12% /boot
$ !u
uptime
12:33:29 up 35 min, 1 user, load average: 0.00, 0.00,
0.00
```

```
$ sudo !w
sudo whoami
root
```

Repeat the Last Command That Started with a given String

```
$ !<string>
```

This is another example of an event designator. To recall the most recent command that begins with <string>, run "!<string>". You can simply specify the first letter, or as much of the string to make it unique. This example demonstrates that concept.

```
$ who
jason          pts/1  2014-04-06 21:04 (192.168.1.117)
$ w
jason          pts/1      192.168.1.117 21:04 0.00s
0.33s 0.00s w
$ !w
w
jason          pts/1      192.168.1.117 21:04 0.00s
0.33s 0.00s w
$ !wh
who
jason          pts/1  2014-04-06 21:04 (192.168.1.117)
```

Here is a practical example where you check to see if a process is running, kill it, and confirm that it did indeed stop.

```
$ ps -fu apache
```

```
UID     PID  PPID  C STIME TTY TIME CMD
apache 1877 1879  0 21:32 ?    00:00:00
/usr/sbin/httpd
apache 1879 1     0 21:32 ?    00:00:00
/usr/sbin/httpd
$ sudo service httpd stop
Stopping httpd:         [  OK  ]
$ !p
ps -fu apache
UID     PID  PPID  C STIME TTY TIME CMD
$
```

Reuse the Second Word (First Argument) from the Previous Command

```
$ !^
```

If you need to grab the second word from the previous command, you can use the "!^" word designator. Wherever you use "!^" it will be replaced by the second word from the previous command. You can also think of this as the first argument to the previous command.

```
$ host www.google.com 8.8.8.8
Using domain server:
Name: 8.8.8.8
Address: 8.8.8.8#53
Aliases:
www.google.com has address 173.194.46.83
www.google.com has address 173.194.46.81
www.google.com has address 173.194.46.84
www.google.com has address 173.194.46.82
```

```
www.google.com has address 173.194.46.80

www.google.com has IPv6 address
2607:f8b0:4009:805::1013

$ ping -c1 !^

ping -c1 www.google.com

PING www.google.com (173.194.46.80) 56(84) bytes of
data.

64 bytes from ord08s11-in-f16.1e100.net
(173.194.46.80): icmp_seq=1 ttl=51 time=17.0 ms

--- www.google.com ping statistics ---

1 packets transmitted, 1 received, 0% packet loss,
time 49ms

rtt min/avg/max/mdev = 17.071/17.071/17.071/0.000 ms

$
```

Reuse the Last Word (Last Argument) from the Previous Command

```
$ !$
```

Quite often I find myself needing to perform another operation on the last item on the previous command line. To access that item in your current command, use "!$".

```
$ unzip tpsreport.zip
Archive: tpsreport.zip
  inflating: cover-sheet.doc
$ rm !$
rm tpsreport.zip
$ mv cover-sheet.doc reports/
$ du -sh !$
```

```
du -sh reports/
4.7G  reports/
$
```

Reuse the Nth Word from a Previous Command

```
$ !!:N
$ <event_designator>:<number>
```

To access a word in the previous command use "!!:N" where N is the number of the word you wish to retrieve. The first word is 0, the second word is 1, etc. You can think of 0 as being the command, 1 as being the first argument to the command, 2 as being the second argument, and so on.

You can use any event designator in conjunction with a word designator. In the following example, "!!" is the most recent command line: avconv -i screencast.mp4 podcast.mp3. The "!a" event designator expands to that same command since it's the most recent command that started with the letter "a."

```
$ avconv -i screencast.mp4 podcast.mp3
$ mv !!:2 converted/
mv screencast.mp4 converted/
$ mv !a:3 podcasts/
mv podcast.mp3 podcasts/
$
```

Repeat the Previous Command While Substituting a String

```
$ ^<string1>^<string2>^
```

This little trick is great for quickly correcting typing mistakes. If you omit ^<string2>^, then <string1> will be removed from the previous command. By default, only the first occurrence of <string1> is replaced. To replace every occurrence, append ":&". You can omit the trailing caret symbol, except when using ":&".

```
$ grpe jason /etc/passwd
-bash: grpe: command not found
$ ^pe^ep
grep jason /etc/passwd
jason:x:501:501:Jason Cannon:/home/jason:/bin/bash
$ grep rooty /etc/passwd
$ ^y
grep root /etc/passwd
root:x:0:0:root:/root:/bin/bash
operator:x:11:0:operator:/root:/sbin/nologin
$ grep canon /etc/passwd ; ls -ld /home/canon
ls: cannot access /home/canon: No such file or
directory
$ ^canon^cannon^:&
grep cannon /etc/passwd ; ls -ld /home/cannon
cannon:x:1001:1001::/home/cannon:/bin/sh
drwxr-xr-x 2 cannon ball 4096 Apr  7 00:22 /home/cannon
```

Reference a Word of the Current Command and Reuse It

```
$ !#:N
```

The "!#" event designator represents the current command line, while the :N word designator represents a word on the command line. Word references are zero based, so the first word, which is almost always a command, is :0, the second word, or first argument to the command, is :1, etc.

```
$ mv Working-with-Files.pdf Chapter-18-!#:1
mv Working-with-Files.pdf Chapter-18-Working-with-
Files.pdf
```

Save a Copy of Your Command Line Session

```
$ script
```

If you want to document what you see on your screen, use the script command. The script command captures everything that is printed on your terminal and saves it to a file. You can provide script a file name as an argument or let it create the default file named typescript.

```
$ script
Script started, file is typescript
$ cd /usr/local/bin
$ sudo ./upgradedb.sh
sudo password for jason:
Starting database upgrade.
...
Database upgrade complete.
$ exit
exit
Script done, file is typescript
$ cat typescript
Script started on Wed 09 Apr 2014 06:30:58 PM EDT
$ cd /usr/local/bin
$ sudo ./upgradedb.sh
sudo password for jason:
```

```
Starting database upgrade.

...

Database upgrade complete.
$ exit
exit
Script done on Wed 09 Apr 2014 06:31:44 PM EDT
$
```

Find out Which Commands You Use Most Often

```
$ history | awk '{print $2}' | sort | uniq -c | sort
-rn | head
```

To get a list of the top ten most used commands in your shell history, use the following command.

```
$ history | awk '{print $2}' | sort | uniq -c | sort
-rn | head
       61 ls
       45 cd
       40 cat
       31 vi
       24 ip
       22 sudo
       22 ssh
       22 ll
       19 rm
       17 find
$
```

Clear Your Shell History

```
$ history -c
```

To clear your shell history, use the -c option to the history command.

```
$ history | tail -5
  966  ls -lR Music/
  967  find Music/ -type f -ls
  968  dstat
  969  sudo vi /etc/motd
  970  cd ..
  971  sudo du -s /home/* | sort -n
$ history -c
$ history
      1  history
$
```

TEXT PROCESSING AND MANIPULATION

Strip out Comments and Blank Lines

```
$ grep -E -v "^#|^$" file
```

To strip out all the noise from a configuration file get rid of the comments and blank lines. These two regexes (regular expressions) do the trick. "^#" matches all lines that begin with a "#". "^$" matches all blank lines. The -E option to grep allows us to use regexes and the -v option inverts the matches.

```
[jason@www conf]$ grep -E -v '^#|^$' httpd.conf |
head
ServerTokens OS
ServerRoot "/etc/httpd"
PidFile run/httpd.pid
Timeout 60
KeepAlive Off
MaxKeepAliveRequests 100
KeepAliveTimeout 15
<IfModule prefork.c>
```

```
StartServers          8

MinSpareServers       5

[jason@www conf]$
```

Use Vim to Edit Files over the Network

```
$ vim scp://remote-host//path/to/file

$ vim scp://remote-user@remote-host//path/to/file
```

If you want to edit a file with vim over SSH, you can let it do the heavy lifting of copying the file back and forth.

```
$ vim scp://linuxserver//home/jason/notes.txt
```

Display Output in a Table

```
$ alias ct='column -t'

$ command | ct
```

Use the column command to format text into multiple columns. By using the -t option, column will count the number of columns the input contains and create a table with that number of columns. This can really make the output of many command easier to read. I find myself using this so often that I created an alias for the command.

```
$ alias ct='column -t'

$ echo -e 'one two\nthree four'

one two

three four

$ echo -e 'one two\nthree four' | ct

one     two
```

```
three four
$ mount -t ext4
/dev/vda2 on / type ext4 (rw)
/dev/vda1 on /boot type ext4 (rw)
$ mount -t ext4 | ct
/dev/vda2  on  /       type  ext4  (rw)
/dev/vda1  on  /boot type  ext4  (rw)
$
```

Grab the Last Word on a Line of Output

```
$ awk '{print $NF}' file
$ cat file | awk '{print $NF}'
```

You can have awk print fields by using $FIELD_NUMBER notation. To print the first field use $1, to print the second use $2, etc. However, if you don't know the number of fields, or don't care to count them, use $NF which represents the total number of fields. Awk separates fields on spaces, but you can use the -F argument to change that behavior. Here is how to print all the shells that are in use on the system. Use a colon as the field separator and then print the last field.

```
$ awk -F: '{print $NF}' /etc/passwd | sort -u
```

If you want to display the shell for each user on the system you can do this.

```
$ awk -F: '{print $1,$NF}' /etc/passwd | sort |
column -t
adm                    /sbin/nologin
```

```
apache            /sbin/nologin
avahi-autoipd     /sbin/nologin
bin               /sbin/nologin
bobb              /bin/bash
. . .
```

View Colorized Output with Less

```
$ ls --color=always | less -R
$ grep --color=always file | less -R
```

Some linux distributions create aliases for ls and grep with the --color=auto option. This causes colors to be used only when the output is going to a terminal. When you pipe the output from ls or grep the color codes aren't emitted. You can force color to always be displayed by ls or grep with --color=always. To have the less command display the raw control characters that create colors, use the -R option.

```
$ grep --color=always -i bob /etc/passwd | less -R
$ ls --color=always -l /etc | less -R
```

Preserve Color When Piping to Grep

```
$ ls -l --color=always | grep --color=never string
```

If you pipe colorized input into grep and grep is an alias with the --color=auto option, grep will discard the color from the input and highlight the string that was grepped for. In order to preserve the colorized input, force grep to not use colors with the --color=never option.

```
$ ls -l --color=always *mp3 | grep --color=never jazz
```

```
-rw-r--r--. 1 jason jason 21267371 Feb 16 11:12 jazz-
album-1.mp3
```

Append Text to a File Using Sudo

```
$ echo text | sudo tee -a file
```

If you have ever tried to append text to a file using redirection following a "sudo echo" command, you quickly find this doesn't work. What happens is the echo statement is executed as root but the redirection occurs as yourself.

```
$ sudo echo "PRODUCTION Environment" >> /etc/motd
-bash: /etc/motd: Permission denied
```

Fortunately, use can use sudo in combination the tee command to append text to a file.

```
$ echo "PRODUCTION Environment" | sudo tee -a
/etc/motd
PRODUCTION Environment
```

Change the Case of a String

```
$ tr [:upper:][:lower:]
$ tr [:lower:][:upper:]
```

When you need to change the case of a string, use the tr command. You can supply ranges to tr like "tr a-z A-Z" or use "tr [:lower:][:upper]".

```
$ ENVIRONMENT=PRODUCTION
```

```
$ DIRECTORY=$(echo $ENVIRONMENT | tr
[:upper:][:lower:])

$ echo $ENVIRONMENT | sudo tee -a /etc/motd

$ tail -1 /etc/motd

PRODUCTION

$ sudo mkdir /var/www/$DIRECTORY

$ sudo tar zxf wwwfiles.tgz -C /var/www/$DIRECTORY
```

Display Your Command Search Path in a Human Readable Format

```
$ echo $PATH | tr ':' '\n'
```

Reading a colon separated list of items isn't as easy for us humans as it is for computers. To substitute new lines for colons, use the tr command.

```
$ echo $PATH
/usr/bin:/bin:/usr/local/bin:/bin:/usr/bin:/usr/local
/sbin:/usr/sbin:/sbin
$ echo $PATH | tr ':' '\n'
/usr/bin
/bin
/usr/local/bin
/bin
/usr/bin
/usr/local/sbin
/usr/sbin
/sbin
```

Create a Text File from the Command Line without

Using an Editor

```
$ cat > file
<ctrl-d>
```

If you need to make a quick note and don't need a full blown text editor, you can simply use cat and redirect the output to a file. Press <ctrl-d> when you're finished to create the file.

```
$ cat > shopping.list
eggs
bacon
coffee
<ctrl-d>
$ cat shopping.list
eggs
bacon
coffee
$
```

Display a Block of Text between Two Strings

```
$ awk '/start-pattern/,/stop-pattern/' file.txt
$ command | awk '/start-pattern/,/stop-pattern/'
```

The grep command is great at extracting a single line of text. But what if you need to capture an entire block of text? Use awk and provide it a start and stop pattern. The pattern can simply be a string or even a regular expression.

```
$ sudo dmidecode | awk /Processor/,/Manuf/
```

```
Processor Information
                Socket Designation: SOCKET 0
                Type: Central Processor
                Family: Core i5
                Manufacturer: Intel
$ awk '/worker.c/,/^$/' httpd.conf
<IfModule worker.c>
StartServers              4
MaxClients                    300
MinSpareThreads          25
MaxSpareThreads          75
ThreadsPerChild          25
MaxRequestsPerChild  0
</IfModule>
$
```

Delete a Block of Text between Two Strings

```
$ sed '/start-pattern/,/stop-pattern/d' file
$ command | sed '/start-pattern/,/stop-pattern/d'
file
```

You can delete a block of text with the sed command by providing it a start and stop pattern and telling it to delete that entire range. The patterns can be strings or regular expressions. This example deletes the the first seven lines since "#" matches the first line and "^$" matches the seventh line.

```
$ cat ports.conf
# If you just change the port or add more ports here,
you will likely also
```

```
# have to change the VirtualHost statement in

# /etc/apache2/sites-enabled/000-default

# This is also true if you have upgraded from before
2.2.9-3 (i.e. from

# Debian etch). See /usr/share/doc/apache2.2-
common/NEWS.Debian.gz and

# README.Debian.gz

NameVirtualHost *:80

Listen 80

<IfModule mod_ssl.c>

        # If you add NameVirtualHost *:443 here, you
will also have to change

        # the VirtualHost statement in
/etc/apache2/sites-available/default-ssl

        # to <VirtualHost *:443>

        # Server Name Indication for SSL named
virtual hosts is currently not

        # supported by MSIE on Windows XP.

        Listen 443

</IfModule>

<IfModule mod_gnutls.c>

        Listen 443

</IfModule>

$ sed '/#/,/^$/d' ports.conf

NameVirtualHost *:80

Listen 80

<IfModule mod_ssl.c>

<IfModule mod_gnutls.c>

        Listen 443

</IfModule>
```

Fix Common Typos with Aliases

```
$ alias typo='correct spelling'
```

If you find yourself repeatedly making the same typing mistake over and over, fix it with an alias.

```
$ grpe root /etc/passwd
bash: grpe: command not found
$ echo "alias grpe='grep'" >> ~/.bash_profile
$ . ~/.bash_profile
$ grpe root /etc/passwd
root:x:0:0:root:/root:/bin/bash
$
```

Sort the Body of Output While Leaving the Header on the First Line Intact

Add this function to your personal initialization files such as ~/.bash_profile:

```
body() {
    IFS= read -r header
    printf '%s\n' "$header"
    "$@"
}
$ command | body sort
$ cat file | body sort
```

I find myself wanting to sort the output of commands that contain headers. After the sort is performed the header ends up sorted right along with the rest of the content. This function will keep the header line intact and allow sorting of the remaining lines of output. Here are some examples to illustrate the usage of this function.

```
$ df -h | sort -k 5
/dev/vda2    28G    3.2G   25G          12%   /
tmpfs              504M   68K    504M   1%          /dev/shm
/dev/vda1    485M   444M   17M          97%   /boot
Filesystem   Size   Used   Avail  Use%  Mounted    on
$ df -h | body sort -k 5
Filesystem   Size   Used   Avail  Use%  Mounted    on
/dev/vda2    28G    3.2G   25G          12%   /
tmpfs              504M   68K    504M   1%          /dev/shm
/dev/vda1    485M   444M   17M          97%   /boot
$ ps -eo pid,%cpu,cmd | head -1
  PID %CPU CMD
$ ps -eo pid,%cpu,cmd | sort -nrk2 | head
  675 12.5 mysqld
  PID %CPU CMD
  994  0.0 /usr/sbin/acpid
  963  0.0 /usr/sbin/modem-manager
  958  0.0 NetworkManager
  946  0.0 dbus-daemon
  934  0.0 /usr/sbin/fcoemon --syslog
  931  0.0 [bnx2fc_thread/0]
  930  0.0 [bnx2fc_l2_threa]
```

```
  929  0.0 [bnx2fc]
$ ps -eo pid,%cpu,cmd | body sort -nrk2 | head
  PID %CPU CMD
  675 12.5 mysqld
  994  0.0 /usr/sbin/acpid
  963  0.0 /usr/sbin/modem-manager
  958  0.0 NetworkManager
  946  0.0 dbus-daemon
  934  0.0 /usr/sbin/fcoemon --syslog
  931  0.0 [bnx2fc_thread/0]
  930  0.0 [bnx2fc_12_threa]
  929  0.0 [bnx2fc]
$
```

Remove a Character or set of Characters from a String or Line of Output

```
$ command | tr -d "X"
$ command | tr -d [SET]
$ cat file | tr -d "X"
$ cat file | tr -d [set]
```

The tr command is typically used to translate characters, but with the -d option it deletes characters. This example shows how to get rid of quotes.

```
$ cat cities.csv
1,"Chicago","USA","IL"
2,"Austin","USA","TX"
3,"Santa Cruz","USA","CA"
```

```
$ cat cities.csv | cut -d, -f2
"Chicago"
"Austin"
"Santa Cruz"
$ cat cities.csv | cut -d, -f2 | tr -d '"'
Chicago
Austin
Santa Cruz
$
```

You can also let tr delete a group of characters. This example removes all the vowels from the output.

```
$ cat cities.csv | cut -d, -f2 | tr -d [aeiou]
"Chcg"
"Astn"
"Snt Crz"
$
```

Count the Number of Occurrences of a String

```
$ uniq -c file
$ command | uniq -c
```

The uniq command omits adjacent duplicate lines from files. Since uniq doesn't examine an entire file or stream of input for unique lines, only unique adjacent lines, it is typically preceded by the sort command via a pipe. You can have the uniq command count the unique occurrences of a string by using the "-c" option. This comes in useful if you are trying to look through log files for occurrences of the same message, PID, status code, username, etc.

Let's find the all of the unique HTTP status codes in an apache web server log file named access.log. To do this, print out the ninth item in the log file with the awk command.

```
$ tail -1 access.log
18.19.20.21 - - [19/Apr/2014:19:51:20 -0400] "GET /
HTTP/1.1" 200 7136 "-" "Mozilla/5.0 (Windows NT 6.1;
WOW64) AppleWebKit/537.36 (KHTML, like Gecko)
Chrome/33.0.1750.154 Safari/537.36"
$ tail -1 access.log | awk '{print $9}'
200
$ awk '{print $9}' access.log | sort | uniq
200
301
302
404
$
```

Let's take it another step forward and count how many of each status code we have.

```
$ awk '{print $9}' access.log | sort | uniq -c | sort
-nr
   5641 200
    207 301
     86 404
     18 302
      2 304
```

$

Now let's see extract the status code and hour from the access.log file and count the unique occurrences of those combinations. Next, lets sort them by number of occurrences. This will show us the hours during which the website was most active.

```
$ cat access.log | awk '{print $9, $4}' | cut -c 1-
4,18-19 | uniq -c | sort -n | tail
       72 200 09
       76 200 06
       81 200 06
       82 200 06
       83 200 06
       83 200 06
       84 200 06
      109 200 20
      122 200 20
      383 200 10
$
```

NETWORKING AND SSH

Serve Files in the Current Directory via a Web Interface

```
$ python -m SimpleHTTPServer
$ python3 -m http.server
```

By default, this command starts a web server and serves up the content in the current directory over port 8000. You can change the port by specifying it at the end of the line. If no index.html file exists in the current directory, then the directory listing is shown. Start the web server and use a web browser to navigate to it. (firefox http://localhost:8000)

This can come in handy when you are working on HTML content and you want to see how it looks in a web browser without installing and configuring a full blown web server.

```
$ python -m SimpleHTTPServer
Serving HTTP on 0.0.0.0 port 8000 …
localhost.localdomain - - [06/Apr/2014 21:49:20] "GET
/ HTTP/1.1" 200 -
```

Here's how to start the web server on the standard HTTP port. Since port 80 is a privileged port, IE it's 1024 or lower, doing this requires root privileges.

```
$ sudo python -m SimpleHTTPServer 80
Serving HTTP on 0.0.0.0 port 80 ...
```

Mount a Directory from a Remote Server on Your Local Host via SSH

```
$ sshfs remote-host:/directory mountpoint
$ fusermount -u mountpiont
```

Sometimes it's easier to work on files and directories if they are, or appear to be, local to your machine. For example, maybe you have a local application that doesn't exist on the server that you use to manipulate files. Instead of downloading the file from the server, modifying it, and and uploading it back to the server, you can mount the remote directory on your local workstation. Here is an example of updating a website over SSH.

```
$ mkdir web-files
$ sshfs www.example.com:/home/jason/public_html
$ bluefish web-files/index.html
$ fusermount -u web-files
```

Just like ssh command, you can use the user@host format if your remote username is different from your local username. Also, if no directory is specified after the colon, then your home directory is assumed.

Get Your Public IP from the Command Line Using Curl

```
$ curl ifconfig.me
```

If you ever need to determine your public (Internet) IP address you can use the ifconfig.me website.

```
$ curl ifconfig.me
198.145.20.140
$ curl ifconfig.me/ip
198.145.20.140
$ curl ifconfig.me/host
pub2.kernel.org
```

SSH into a Remote System without a Password

```
$ ssh-keygen
$ ssh-copy-id remote-host
$ ssh remote-host
```

In order to SSH into a remote host without a password you'll need an SSH key pair consisting of a private and public key. On the remote host the contents of the public key need to be in ~/.ssh/authorized_keys. The ssh-copy-id script performs that work.

If you want to generate a key without a password, simply hit enter when prompted for a passphrase. You can optionally supply a blank string to the -N option. (ssh-keygen -N ")

```
$ ssh-keygen
Generating public/private rsa key pair.
```

```
Enter file in which to save the key
(/home/jason/.ssh/id_rsa):

Enter passphrase (empty for no passphrase):

Enter same passphrase again:

Your identification has been saved in
/home/jason/.ssh/id_rsa.

Your public key has been saved in
/home/jason/.ssh/id_rsa.pub.

The key fingerprint is:

0d:2e:e4:32:dd:da:60:a5:2e:0f:c5:89:d5:78:30:ad
jason@laptop.localdomain

The key's randomart image is:

+--[ RSA 2048]----+
|         o.      |
|          =.     |
|         +.=     |
|        BEB o    |
|       + @ S .   |
|        * =      |
|         o o .   |
|          +      |
|           .     |
+-----------------+

$ ssh-copy-id linuxserver

jason@192.168.122.60's password:

Now try logging into the machine, with "ssh
'linuxserver'", and check in:

  .ssh/authorized_keys

to make sure we haven't added extra keys that you
weren't expecting.
```

```
$ ssh linuxserver
$ hostname
linuxserver
$
```

Show Open Network Connections

```
$ sudo lsof -Pni
```

The lsof command can not only be used to display open files, but open network ports, and network connections. The -P option prevents the conversion of port numbers to port names. The -n option prevents the conversion of IP addresses to host names. The -i option tells lsof to display network connections.

```
$ sudo lsof -Pni
COMMAND           PID  USER   FD    TYPE DEVICE SIZE/OFF
NODE NAME
dhclient          989  root         6u   IPv4  11522
0t0   UDP *:68
sshd             1202  root         3u   IPv4  12418
0t0   TCP *:22 (LISTEN)
sshd             1202  root         4u   IPv6  12423
0t0   TCP *:22 (LISTEN)
ntpd             1210   ntp   16u  IPv4  12464
0t0   UDP *:123
ntpd             1210   ntp   17u  IPv6  12465
0t0   UDP *:123
ntpd             1210   ntp   18u  IPv4  12476
0t0   UDP 127.0.0.1:123
ntpd             1210   ntp   19u  IPv4  12477
0t0   UDP 192.168.122.60:123
```

```
ntpd            1210    ntp    20u   IPv6   12478
0t0   UDP  [::1]:123

ntpd            1210    ntp    21u   IPv6   12479
0t0   UDP  [fe80::5054:ff:fe52:d858]:123

master          1364   root    12u   IPv4   12761
0t0   TCP  127.0.0.1:25  (LISTEN)

clock-app 12174 jason    21u   IPv4   78889            0t0
TCP 192.168.122.60:39021->184.25.102.40:80
(ESTABLISHED)

sshd            12339   root          3r   IPv4   74023
0t0   TCP  192.168.122.60:22->192.168.122.1:34483
(ESTABLISHED)

sshd            12342 jason           3u   IPv4   74023
0t0   TCP  192.168.122.60:22->192.168.122.1:34483
(ESTABLISHED)

$
```

Compare the Differences between a Remote and Local File

```
$ ssh remote-host cat /path/to/remotefile | diff
/path/to/localfile -
```

To display the differences between a local and remote file, cat a file over ssh and pipe the output into a diff or sdiff command. The diff and sdiff commands can accept standard input in lieu of a file by supplying it a dash for one of the file names.

```
$ ssh linuxsvr cat /etc/passwd | diff /etc/passwd -
32c32

< terry:x:503:1000::/home/terry:/bin/ksh

---

> terry:x:503:1000::/home/terry:/bin/bash
```

```
35a36
> bob:x:1000:1000:Bob Smith:/home/bob:/bin/bash
$
```

Send Email from the Command Line

```
$ mail recipient@domain.com
$ echo 'message' | mail -s 'subject'
recipient@domain.com
```

To send an email use the mail command. You can enter in a message interactively or via a pipe. End your interactive message with ctrl-d.

```
$ mail jim@mycorp.com
Subject: Message from the command line
Isn't this great?

EOT
$ echo "Here's the lazy way" | mail -s 'Message from
the command line' jim@mycorp.com
```

Send an Email Attachment from the Command Line

```
$ mail -a /path/to/attachment
$ echo 'message' | mail -s 'subject' -a
/path/to/attachment recipient@domain.com
```

If you ever need to send an email attachment from the command line, use the -a option to the mail command.

```
$ echo "Here is the file you requested" | mail -s
"The file" -a /tmp/files.tgz jim@mycorp.com
$
```

Create an SSH Tunnel to Access Remote Resources

```
$ ssh -N -L local-port:host:remote-port remote-host
```

To create an SSH tunnel, use the -L option. The first port is the port that will be opened on your local machine. Connections to this port will be tunneled through remote-host and sent to the host and remote port specified in the -L option. The -N option tells SSH to not execute a command -- your shell -- on the remote host.

Let's say you want to access a website that isn't available on the internet, but is accessible from a server that you have SSH access to. You can create a tunnel that allows you to browse that website like you were behind the company's firewall. This command will forward any connections from your local machine on port 8000 through the jump server to the intranet server on port 80. Point your web browser to http://localhost:8000 and start surfing.

```
$ ssh -N -L 8000:intranet.acme.com:80 jump-server &
[1] 23253
$ firefox http://localhost:8000
```

Another use case is to access a service that is running on a server that you have SSH access to. If you need access to a mysql server that only allows database connections from specific hosts, you can create an SSH tunnel for your connection. Since the mysql service is running on localhost:3306 of the remote machine, the -L option would look like this: -L 3306:localhost:3306. You can use the mysql command line client on your local machine to connect to the database, but what's even more interesting is to use graphical desktop applications that aren't available on the server. For example, you could use this tunnel and connect to the database with MySQL Workbench, Navicat, or some other application.


```
$ ssh -N -L 3306:localhost:3306 db01 &
[1] 13455
$ mysql -h 127.0.0.1
Welcome to the MySQL monitor.  Commands end with ; or
\g.
Your MySQL connection id is 9
Server version: 5.1.73 Source distribution
Copyright (c) 2000, 2013, Oracle and/or its
affiliates. All rights reserved.
Oracle is a registered trademark of Oracle
Corporation and/or its
affiliates. Other names may be trademarks of their
respective
owners.
Type 'help;' or '\h' for help. Type '\c' to clear the
current input statement.
mysql>
```

Find out Which Programs Are Listening on Which Ports

```
$ sudo netstat -nutlp
```

Here are the descriptions of the netstat options used in order to get a list of programs and the ports that they are listening on.

-n show numerical addresses instead of determining symbolic names

-u include the UDP protocol

-t include the TCP protocol

-l show only listening sockets

-p show the PID and program name

```
$  sudo netstat -nutlp

Active Internet connections (only servers)

Proto Recv-Q Send-Q Local Address  Foreign Address
State   PID/Program name
tcp            0            0   0.0.0.0:3306
0.0.0.0:*       LISTEN  4546/mysqld

tcp            0            0   0.0.0.0:22
0.0.0.0:*       LISTEN  1161/sshd

tcp            0            0   127.0.0.1:25
0.0.0.0:*       LISTEN  1325/master

tcp            0            0   :::80          :::*
LISTEN   4576/httpd

tcp            0            0   :::22          :::*
LISTEN   1161/sshd

udp            0            0   0.0.0.0:68
0.0.0.0:*                 1008/dhclient

$
```

Use a Different SSH Key for a given Remote Host

Put the following in the ~/.ssh/config file.

```
Host remote-host

IdentityFile ~/.ssh/id_rsa-remote-host
```

If you need or want to use different SSH keys for different hosts, you can explicitly specify them on the command line with the -i option to ssh.

```
$ ssh -i ~/.ssh/id_rsa-db1 db1.example.com
```

If you want to forego specifying the key each time you can create an entry in your ~/.ssh/config file and specify the key there.

```
$ cat ~/.ssh/config
```

```
Host db1.example.com
        IdentityFile ~/.ssh/id_rsa-db1
$ ssh db1.example.com
```

You can use wildcards in the host specification.

```
$ cat~/.ssh/config
Host db*
        IdentityFile ~/.ssh/id_rsa-db1
Host *.work.net
        IdentityFile ~/work-files/keys/id_rsa
$ ssh jim@jumpbox.work.net
```

If you name your SSH keys after the fully qualified domain names of the hosts they relate to, you can use the %h escape character to simplify your ~/.ssh/config file. Instead of having a host entry for each and every server, the %h syntax expands to the fully qualified domain name of the host your are connecting to.

```
$ cat ~/.ssh/config
Host *.example.com
IdentityFile ~/.ssh/id_rsa-%h
$ ls -1 ~/.ssh/id_rsa-*
id_rsa-lax-db-01.example.com
id_rsa-lax-db-01.example.com.pub
id_rsa-lax-web-01.example.com
id_rsa-lax-web-01.example.com.pub
$ ssh lax-db-01.example.com
```

Avoid Having to Type Your Username When Connecting via SSH

Put the following in the ~/.ssh/config file.

```
Host remote-host
User username
```

If you have a different username on your local Linux machine than you do on the remote linux machine, you have to specify it when connecting via SSH. It looks like this.

```
$ ssh jim@server1.example.com
```

To avoid having to type "username@" each time, add a host entry to your ~/.ssh/config file.

```
Host server1.example.com
        User jim
```

Once your have configured the host entry, you can simply ssh into the remote host.

```
$ whoami
james
$ ssh server1.example.com
$ whoami
jim
$
```

Simplify Multi-Hop SSH Connections and Transparently Proxy SSH Connections

Put the following in the ~/.ssh/config file.

```
Host jumphost.example.com

  ProxyCommand none

Host *.example.com

  ProxyCommand ssh -W %h:%p jumphost.example.com
```

If you need to access a host that sits behind an SSH gateway server or jump server, you can make your life easier by telling SSH to automatically use the SSH gateway when you connect to the final remote host. Instead of first connecting to the gateway and then entering another ssh command to connect to the destination host, you simply type "ssh destination-host" from your local machine. Using the above configuration, this command will proxy your ssh connection to server1 through jumphost.

```
$ ssh server1.example.com
$ uname -n
server1
$
```

Disconnect from a Remote Session and Reconnect at a Later Time, Picking up Where You Left Off

```
$ ssh remote-host
$ screen
ctrl-a, d
$ exit
```

```
$ ssh remote-host
$ screen -r
```

When I have a long running process that I need to complete on a remote host, I always start a screen session before launching that process. I don't want a blip in my network connection to interrupt the work being performed on the remote host. Sometimes I launch a process, detach from the session, and reconnect later to examine all the output that occurred while I was away.

First, ssh into the remote host. Next, start a screen session. Start performing your work on the remote host. Detach from the screen session by typing ctrl-a followed by d. The process you started will still be running in the screen session while you're away. Also, any output generated will be available for you to view at a later time.

```
$ ssh remote-host
$ screen
$ /usr/local/bin/migrate-db
Starting DB migration at Sun Apr 13 21:02:50 EDT 2014
<ctrl-a,d>
[detached]
$ exit
```

To reconnect to your screen session, connect to the remote host and type screen -r. If there is any output that scrolled past the top of the screen, you can view by typing ctrl-a followed by the escape key. Now use the vi navigation key bindings to view the output history. For example, you can type k to move up one line or ctrl-b to page up. Once you are finished looking at the output history, hit escape to return to the live session. To quit your screen session, type exit.

```
$ ssh remote-host
$ screen -r
Starting DB migration at 21:02
table1 migrated at 21:34
table2 migrated at 22:11
table3 migrated at 22:54
DB migration completed at 23:04
$ exit
[screen is terminating]
$ exit
```

Screen is one of the most widely used and readily available screen multiplexers. However, there are alternatives such as tmux, dtach, and byobu.

Configure SSH to Append Domain Names to Host Names Based on a Pattern

The contents of ~/.ssh/config:

```
host-prefix* !*.domain.com
        HostName %h.domain.com
```

If you connect to hosts in multiple domains via ssh it can get tiresome typing out the fully qualified domain name each time. One way around this problem is to add each domain to the search list in /etc/resolv.conf. The resolver will the attempt the resolution for the specified host name in each of the domains in the search list until it finds one that resolves.

```
$ cat /etc/resolv.conf
```

```
nameserver 8.8.8.8
nameserver 8.8.4.4
search domain1.com domain2.com domain3.com
domain4.com domain5.com domain6.com domain7.com
```

When typing "ssh remote-host" with the above resolv.conf in place, the resolver will attempt to translate remote-host.domain1.com into an IP address. If that fails, it will attempt to resolve remote-host.domain2.com, etc. The problem with the above reslov.conf is that the search list is limited to just six domains. So, remote-host.domain7.com is never attempted. Additionally, the search list is limited to 256 characters, regardless the number of domains.

How can you get around the six domain search list limit? If you're lucky enough to have a pattern of hostnames that correlate with domain names, you can configure ssh to do the resolution. For example, for FQDNs like "ny-www1.newyork.company.com" and "ny-mysql-07.newyork.company.com" you can create a rule that appends ".newyork.company.com" to any host that begins with "ny." You'll also want to tell ssh to ignore any hosts that begin with "ny" that already have ".newyork.company.com" appended to them. Here's an example ~/.ssh/config file that does that.

```
$ cat ~/.ssh/config
ny* !*.newyork.company.com
        HostName %h.newyork.company.com
db* !*.databases.company.com
        HostName %h.databases.company.com
jump* !*.company.com
        HostName %h.company.com
```

Now when you type "ssh ny-test" ssh will attempt to connect to "ny-test.newyork.company.com." For hosts that begin with "db," ssh will append ".databases.company.com" to the host name. Hosts the begin with "jump" will have the ".company.com" domain name appened to them.

```
$ ssh ny-www1
$ hostname -f
ny-www1.newyork.company.com
$ exit
$ ssh jump-ny-01
$ hostname -f
jump-ny-01.company.com
$ exit
$
```

Run a Command Immune to Hangups, Allowing the Job to Run after You Disconnect

```
$ nohup command &
```

Normally when you start a job in the background and log out of your session the job gets killed. One way to ensure a command keeps running after you disconnect from the host is to use the nohup command. No hup stands for no hang up. By default the output of the command is stored in a file named "nohup.out" in the directory the program was launched in. You can examine the contents of this file later to see the output of the command. To use a different filename, employ redirection.

```
$ ssh db-server
```

```
$ nohup /usr/local/bin/upgradedb.sh  &
[1] 13370
$ exit
$ ssh db-server
$ cat nohup.out
Starting database upgrade.
...
Database upgrade complete.
$ nohup /usr/local/bin/post-upgrade.sh >
/tmp/post.log &
[1] 16711
$ exit
$ ssh db-server
$ cat /tmp/post.log
Post processing completed.
$
```

Encrypt Your Web Browsing Data with an SSH SOCKS Proxy

```
$ ssh -D PORT remote-host
```

If you are using an open wireless hotspot and want to ensure your web browsing data is encrypted, you can redirect your web browsing traffic through another host via SSH. Start ssh with the "-D" option and provide a port to open up on your local computer for proxy connections. If you only want to perform the port forwarding and not actually log into the shell of the remote host, use the "-N" option for ssh. Configure your web browser to use a SOCKS 5 proxy using localhost for the host and the port you supplied to ssh.

```
$ ssh -ND 1080 ubuntu@ec2-75-101-157-145.compute-
1.amazonaws.com

$ firefox http://www.mybank.com
```

Download a Webpage, HTTP Data, or Use a Web API from the Command Line

```
$ curl -o file.html http://website/webpage

$ wget http://website/webpage
```

The curl and wget commands can be used to download a webpage or anything that is available on a web server. You can use these commands to interact with HTTP APIs, download software packages, download a status page, or even get the current weather.

Here's an example of checking the status page of your local apache web server.

```
$ curl -o server-status.html http://localhost/server-
status

  % Total        % Received % Xferd  Average Speed
Time         Time          Time  Current

                                    Dload   Upload
Total    Spent        Left  Speed
100  6148  100  6148         0        0  1070k
0 --:--:-- --:--:-- --:--:-- 1200k

$ wget http://localhost/server-status

--2014-04-19 14:37:18--  http://localhost/server-
status

Resolving localhost (localhost)... 127.0.0.1

Connecting to localhost (localhost)|127.0.0.1|:80...
connected.

HTTP request sent, awaiting response... 200 OK
```

```
Length: 6377 (6.2K) [text/html]

Saving to: `server-status'

100%[=====>] 6,377            --.-K/s   in 0s

2014-04-19 14:37:18 (105 MB/s) - `server-status'
saved [6377/6377]

$ grep uptime server-status*

server-status:<dt>Server uptime:   50 minutes 13
seconds</dt>

server-status.html:<dt>Server uptime:   50 minutes 5
seconds</dt>
```

Here's an example of getting the current weather.

```
$ curl -so lax-weather.html \

http://weather.noaa.gov/pub/data/observations/metar/d
ecoded/KLAX.TXT

$ cat lax-weather.html

LOS ANGELES INTERNTL AIRPORT, CA, United States
(KLAX) 33-56N 118-23W 46M

Apr 19, 2014 - 02:53 PM EDT / 2014.04.19 1853 UTC

Wind: from the W (260 degrees) at 10 MPH (9 KT):0

Visibility: 10 mile(s):0

Sky conditions: mostly cloudy

Temperature: 64.9 F (18.3 C)

Dew Point: 54.0 F (12.2 C)

Relative Humidity: 67%

Pressure (altimeter): 30.03 in. Hg (1016 hPa)

ob: KLAX 191853Z 26009KT 10SM FEW022 BKN220 18/12
A3003 RMK AO2 SLP167 T01830122

cycle: 19
```

```
$ wget -q \
http://weather.noaa.gov/pub/data/observations/metar/d
ecoded/KLAX.TXT
$ cat KLAX.TXT
LOS ANGELES INTERNTL AIRPORT, CA, United States
(KLAX) 33-56N 118-23W 46M
Apr 19, 2014 - 02:53 PM EDT / 2014.04.19 1853 UTC
Wind: from the W (260 degrees) at 10 MPH (9 KT):0
Visibility: 10 mile(s):0
Sky conditions: mostly cloudy
Temperature: 64.9 F (18.3 C)
Dew Point: 54.0 F (12.2 C)
Relative Humidity: 67%
Pressure (altimeter): 30.03 in. Hg (1016 hPa)
ob: KLAX 191853Z 26009KT 10SM FEW022 BKN220 18/12
A3003 RMK AO2 SLP167 T01830122
cycle: 19
$
```

Download and install a package.

```
$ wget -q \
https://download.elasticsearch.org/elasticsearch/elas
ticsearch/elasticsearch-1.1.1.deb
$ sudo dpkg -i elasticsearch-1.1.1.deb
Selecting previously unselected package
elasticsearch.
(Reading database ... 162097 files and directories
currently installed.)
Unpacking elasticsearch (from elasticsearch-
```

```
1.1.1.deb) ...

Setting up elasticsearch (1.1.1) ...

Adding system user `elasticsearch' (UID 116) ...

Adding new user `elasticsearch' (UID 116) with group
`elasticsearch' ...

Not creating home directory
`/usr/share/elasticsearch'.

### NOT starting elasticsearch by default on bootup,
please execute

 sudo update-rc.d elasticsearch defaults 95 10

### In order to start elasticsearch, execute

 sudo /etc/init.d/elasticsearch start

Processing triggers for ureadahead ...

$ sudo /etc/init.d/elasticsearch start

 * Starting Elasticsearch Server
[ OK ]

$
```

Interact with a web API.

```
$ curl http://localhost:9200
{

  "status" : 200,

  "name" : "NFL Superpro",

  "version" : {

        "number" : "1.1.1",

        "build_hash" : "f1585f096d3f3985e73456dcc",

        "build_timestamp" : "2014-04-16T14:27:12Z",

        "build_snapshot" : false,
```

```
        "lucene_version" : "4.7"
    },
    "tagline" : "You Know, for Search"
}
$ curl http://localhost:9200/_cluster/health?pretty
{
    "cluster_name" : "elasticsearch",
    "status" : "green",
    "timed_out" : false,
    "number_of_nodes" : 1,
    "number_of_data_nodes" : 1,
    "active_primary_shards" : 0,
    "active_shards" : 0,
    "relocating_shards" : 0,
    "initializing_shards" : 0,
    "unassigned_shards" : 0
}
$
```

Use Vim to Edit Files over the Network

```
$ vim scp://remote-host//path/to/file
$ vim scp://remote-user@remote-host//path/to/file
```

If you want to edit a file with vim over SSH, you can let it do the heavy lifting of copying the file back and forth.

```
$ vim scp://linuxserver//home/jason/notes.txt
```

SHELL SCRIPTING

Use a for Loop at the Command Line

```
$ for VAR in LIST
> do
>   # use $VAR
> done
```

When you need to perform the same action for a list of items, you can use a for loop right from your shell.

```
$ for USER in bob jill fred
> do
>   sudo passwd -l $USER
>   logger -t naughty-user $USER
> done
Locking password for user bob.
passwd: Success
Locking password for user jill.
passwd: Success
```

```
Locking password for user fred.
passwd: Success
$ sudo tail -3 /var/log/messages
Apr  8 19:29:03 linuxserver naughty-user: bob
Apr  8 19:29:03 linuxserver naughty-user: jill
Apr  8 19:29:03 linuxserver naughty-user: fred
```

You can also type entire loop on one command line

```
$ for USER in bob jill fred; do sudo passwd -l $USER;
logger -t naughty-user $USER; done
...
```

Command Substitution

```
$ VAR=`command`
$ VAR=$(command)
```

There are two forms of command substitution. The first form uses backticks (`) to surround a command while the second form uses a dollar sign followed by parenthesis that surround a command. They are functionally equivalent with the backtick form being the older style. The output of the command can be used as an argument to another command, to set a variable, or for generating the argument list for a for loop.

```
$ EXT_FILESYSTEMS=$(grep ext fstab |awk '{print $2}')
$ echo $EXT_FILESYSTEMS
/ /boot
$ cp file.txt file.txt.`date +%F`
```

```
$ ls file.txt*

file.txt   file.txt.2014-04-08

$ ps -fp $(cat /var/run/ntpd.pid)

UID             PID  PPID  C STIME TTY              TIME
CMD

ntp            1210         1  0 Apr06 ?
00:00:05 ntpd -u ntp:ntp -p /var/run/ntpd

$ sudo kill -9 $(cat /var/run/ntpd.pid)

$ for x in $(cut -d: -f1 /etc/passwd); do groups $x;
done

jason : jason sales

bobdjr : sales

jim : jim
```

Store Command Line Output as a Variable to Use Later

```
$ for VAR in LIST

> do

>   VAR2=$(command)

>   VAR3=$(command)

>   echo "$VAR2 VAR3"

> done
```


Command substitution can be used to assign values to variables. If you need to reuse the output of a command multiple times, assign it to a variable once and reuse the variable. This example shows how the output of the id command is used multiple times in one script.


```
$ for USER in $(cut -f1 -d: /etc/passwd)

> do

>   UID_MIN=$(grep ^UID_MIN /etc/login.defs | awk
```

```
'{print $NF}')
>   USERID=$(id -u $USER)
>   [ $USERID -lt $UID_MIN ] || {
>           echo "Forcing password expiration for $USER
with UID of $USERID."
>           sudo passwd -e $USER
>   }
> done
Forcing password expiration for bob with UID of 1000.
Forcing password expiration for bobdjr with UID of
1001.
Forcing password expiration for bobh with UID of
1002.
```

Read in Input One Line at a Time

```
$ while read LINE
> do
>   # Do something with $LINE
> done < file.txt
$ command | while read LINE
> do
>   # Do something with $LINE
> done
```

If you want to iterate over a list of words, use a for loop. If you want to iterate over a line, use a while loop in combination with a read statement and redirection.

Let's look for file systems that are over 90% utilized. If we try to use an if statement it will break up the output into word chunks like this.

```
$ df | head -1
Filesystem 1K-blocks Used Available Use% Mounted on
$ for x in $(df)
> do
> echo $x
> done
Filesystem
1K-blocks
Used
Available
Use%
Mounted
on
...
```

We need to read in entire lines at a time like this.

```
$ df | while read LINE
> do
> echo $LINE
> done
Filesystem 1K-blocks Used Available Use% Mounted on
...
```

Here is one way to find file systems that are over 90% utilized.

```
$ df

Filesystem 1K-blocks Used Available Use% Mounted on

/dev/sda2   28891260 3270340       25327536   12% /

tmpfs         515320       72       515248    1% /dev/shm

/dev/sda1     495844   453683              16561   97% /boot

$ df | grep [0-9]% | while read LINE

> do

>    use=$(echo $LINE | awk '{print $5}' | tr -d '%')

>    mountpoint=$(echo $LINE | awk '{print $6}')

> [ $use -gt 90 ] && echo "$mountpoint is over 90%
utilized."

> done

/boot is over 90% utilized.

$
```

Instead of assigning variables within the while loop, you can assign them with the read statement. Here is how this method looks.

```
$ df | grep [0-9]% | while read fs blocks used
available use mountpoint

> do

>    use=$(echo $use | tr -d '%')

>    [ $use -gt 90 ] && echo "$mountpoint is over 90%
utilized."

> done

/boot is over 90% utilized.
```

Accept User Input and Store It in a Variable

```
$ read VAR
```

```
$ read -n 1 VAR
$ read -p "Prompt text" VAR
```

To accept user input from a user, use the read command. Read will accept an entire line of input and store it into a variable. You can force read to only read a limited number of characters by using the -n option. Instead of using echo statements before a read command, you can supply a prompt by using the -p option. Here is a sample script that uses these techniques.

The contents of backup.sh:

```
#!/bin/bash
while true
do
   read -p "What server would you like to backup? "
SERVER
   echo "Backing up $SERVER"
   /usr/local/bin/backup $SERVER
   read -p "Backup another server? (y/n) " -n 1
BACKUP_AGAIN
   echo
   [ "$BACKUP_AGAIN" = "y" ] || break
done
```

```
$ ./backup.sh
What server would you like to backup? thor
Backing up thor
Backup another server? (y/n) y
```

```
What server would you like to backup? loki

Backing up loki

Backup another server? (y/n) n

$
```

Sum All the Numbers in a given Column of a Text

```
$ awk '{ sum += $1 } END { print sum }' file
$ cat file| awk '{ sum += $1 } END { print sum }
```

Awk can be used to tally up a column of values. You can use this trick to add up all the disk space used across all the file systems on a given system, for example.

```
$ df -mt ext4
Filesystem 1M-blocks Used Available Use% Mounted on
/dev/sda2  28215   3285           24644  12% /
/dev/sda1    485     55            406  12% /boot
$ df -mt ext4 | awk '{ sum += $3 } END {print sum}'
3340
$ sudo dmidecode --type memory
           Size: No Module Installed
           Size: 4096 MB
           Size: No Module Installed
           Size: 4096 MB
$ sudo dmidecode --type memory | grep 'Size:' | awk
'{sum+=$2} END {print sum}'
8192
$
```

Automatically Answer Yes to Any Command

```
$ yes | command
$ yes "string" | command
```

If you are trying to automate a process that requires user input, check out the yes command. By default yes simply prints out "y" until it is killed. You can make yes repeat any string. If you wanted to automatically answer "no" you could run "yes no."

```
$ ./install-my-app.sh
Are you sure you want to install my-app? (y/n) y
Ok, my-app installed.
$ yes | ./install-my-app.sh
Ok, my-app installed.
$
```

SYSTEM ADMINISTRATION

Display Mounted File Systems in a Tabular Format

```
$ mount | column -t
```

The output of the mount command is not formatted in an easy-to-read manner. To make each column line up, pipe the output of the mount command to "column -t". By default mount displays all mounted filesystems, even the pseudo-filesystems like /proc and /sys. To limit output to a filesystem type, use the -t option and provide a type.

```
$ mount -t ext4
/dev/mapper/sys-lv_root  on / type  ext4  (rw)
/dev/sda1 on  /boot  type  ext4  (rw)
$ mount -t ext4 | column -t
/dev/mapper/sys-lv_root on  /      type ext4 (rw)
/dev/sda1               on  /boot type ext4 (rw)
```

Kill All Processes for a given User or Program

```
$ pkill -9 command
$ pkill -9 -u user command
```

If you need to kill several processes with the same command, use the pkill command. If you only want to kill processes for a given user, use the -u option. Pkill will only kill the processes when all the criteria match. That means you can kill all of a given process that is being run by a specific user.

```
$ ps -ef| grep http | grep -v grep
root          12253         1  0 10:55 ?
00:00:00 /usr/sbin/httpd
apache     12255 12253  0 10:55 ?              00:00:00
/usr/sbin/httpd
apache     12256 12253  0 10:55 ?              00:00:00
/usr/sbin/httpd
apache     12257 12253  0 10:55 ?              00:00:00
/usr/sbin/httpd
apache     12258 12253  0 10:55 ?              00:00:00
/usr/sbin/httpd
apache     12259 12253  0 10:55 ?              00:00:00
/usr/sbin/httpd
apache     12260 12253  0 10:55 ?              00:00:00
/usr/sbin/httpd
apache     12261 12253  0 10:55 ?              00:00:00
/usr/sbin/httpd
apache     12262 12253  0 10:55 ?              00:00:00
/usr/sbin/httpd
```

```
$ sudo pkill -9 httpd

$ ps -ef| grep http | grep -v grep

$ ps -ef| grep ssh | grep -v grep

root          1202        1  0 Apr06 ?
00:00:00 /usr/sbin/sshd

root         12339 1202  0 11:22 ?
00:00:00 sshd: jason [priv]

jason        12342 12339  0 11:22 ?
00:00:00 sshd: jason@pts/0

root         12368 1202  1 11:23 ?
00:00:00 sshd: bob [priv]

bob          12372 12368  0 11:23 ?
00:00:00 sshd: bob@pts/1

$ sudo killall -u bob sshd

$ ps -ef| grep ssh | grep -v grep

root          1202        1  0 Apr06 ?
00:00:00 /usr/sbin/sshd

root         12339 1202  0 11:22 ?
00:00:00 sshd: jason [priv]

jason        12342 12339  0 11:22 ?
00:00:00 sshd: jason@pts/0

$
```

Repeat a Command until It Succeeds

```
$ while true

> do

>   command && break

> done
```

The while loop will continue until the condition is false or it encounters a break. In his case we effectively create an infinite loop and break once our chosen command succeeds. If you want to keep pinging a host until it responds, you could use this while loop.

```
$ while true
> do
>    ping -c1 -W1 remote-host >/dev/null 2>&1 && break
> done ; echo "Remote-host is up at $(date)."
Remote-host is up at Fri Apr 11 21:30:29 EDT 2014.
$
```

If you're waiting for a file to show up on your server, you could use this while loop.

```
$ while true
> do
>  ls /svr/ftp/incoming/payroll.txt.gpg 2>/dev/null
&& break
> done; echo "Payroll file arrived at $(date)."
Payroll file arrived at Fri Apr 11 21:33:23 EDT 2014.
```

Find Who Is Using the Most Disk Space

```
$ sudo du -s /home | sort -n
```

This command will display the person who is using the most disk space in their home directory. The users will little disk space will be displayed at the top of your screen and the users using the most disk space will be displayed at the bottom.

```
$ sudo du -s /home/* | sort -n
32      /home/pat
32      /home/terry
40      /home/jim
40      /home/jimbob
44      /home/oracle
19184      /home/adminuser
22208      /home/bob
65132      /home/jason
$
```

If you are looking for a more graphical way to display disk usage, check out the neat utility ncdu.

```
$ ncdu /home
ncdu 1.10 ~ Use the arrow keys to navigate, press ?
for help
--- /home ------------------------------------
37.9GiB [##########] /ryan
 1.3MiB [                    ] /lucas
Total disk usage:  37.9GiB  Apparent size:  37.8GiB
Items: 156055
```

Find the Files That Are Using the Most Disk Space

```
$ find / -type f -exec wc -c {} \; | sort -n
```

Use find to execute the "wc -c" command against each file, revealing it's size in bytes, and then sort that output. The smallest files will be displayed first, and the largest files will be displayed last. If you are scanning every file on a system, this command could take awhile to complete.

```
$ sudo find /var -xdev -type f -exec wc -c {} \; |
sort -n
0 /var/cache/apt/archives/lock
...
2572437 /var/lib/dpkg/available-old
2573098 /var/lib/dpkg/available
38433001 /var/cache/apt/pkgcache.bin
39872802 49659904 /var/cache/apt-xapian-
index/index.1/termlist.DB
62783488 /var/cache/apt-xapian-
index/index.1/postlist.DB
$
```

List Processes, Sorted by Memory Usage

```
$ ps aux | sort -nk 4
```

Use this command to find the processes that are consuming the most memory. The processes using the least amount of memory will scroll off the top of your screen and the ones consuming the most amount of memory will be just above your shell prompt.

In this example, mysqld is consuming 1.3% of the memory on this host.

```
$ ps aux| head -1
USER   PID  %CPU %MEM       VSZ   RSS  TTY    STAT
START  TIME COMMAND
$ ps aux | sort -nk 4 | tail -5
```

```
root  2969  0.0  0.3  11856  3228 ?      Ss   17:16
0:00 sshd: jason [priv]

root  4576  0.0  0.3  11364  3380 ?      Ss   17:52
0:00 /usr/sbin/httpd

root   958  0.0  0.3  20844  4084 ?      Ssl  00:00
0:00 NetworkManager

68    1003  0.0  0.4  17104  4268 ?      Ssl  00:00
0:00 hald

mysql 4546  0.0  1.3 136332 13848 pts/0 Sl   17:52
0:01 /usr/libexec/mysqld

$
```

List Processes, Sorted by CPU Usage

```
$ ps aux | sort -nk 3
```

Use this command to find the processes that are consuming the most CPU. The processes using the least amount of CPU will scroll off the top of your screen and the ones consuming the most amount of CPU will be just above your shell prompt.

In this example, mysqld is consuming 94% of the CPU on this host.

```
$ ps aux| head -1
USER  PID  %CPU %MEM       VSZ   RSS  TTY  STAT
START  TIME COMMAND
$ ps aux | sort -nk 4 | tail -5
root  2469  0.0  0.3  11856    3228 ?    Ss   17:16
0:00 /usr/sbin/fcoemon

root   452  0.0  0.3  20844    4084 ?    Ssl  00:00
0:00 master

root  5571  2.1  0.3  11364    3380 ?    Ss   17:52
0:00 /usr/sbin/httpd
```

66

```
mysql 4447  94 12.8 2134672 1031064 ?   S1   10:52
27:39 /usr/libexec/mysqld
$
```

Quickly Tell If You Are on a 32 Bit or 64 Bit System

```
$ getconf LONG_BIT
```

If you're on a system and need to know if it's 32 or 64 bit, use getconf.

```
$ getconf LONG_BIT
32
$ ssh remote-host getconf LONG_BIT
64
```

Generate a Random Password

```
$ openssl rand -base64 48 | cut -c1-PASSWORD_LENGTH
$ gpw () {  openssl rand -base64 48 | cut -c1-${1}; }
```

You can use the openssl command to generate a random password. If you find yourself doing this often, you can create a function. Simply pass in how long you want the password to be.

```
$ echo 'gpw () {openssl rand -base64 48|cut -c1-${1};
}' >> ~/.bash_profile
$ . ~/.bash_profile
$ gpw
t3eyxkXBHAzb3VdR7G8NV3fMvZpXLOvT+AQwgQnw9pLm/UaRNHcPB
jKaQsr26i3k
$ gpw 6
uu1ZMb
```

FILES AND DIRECTORIES

Quickly Make a Backup of a File

```
$ cp file{,.bak}
```

You can use brace expansion to quickly create a backup copy of a file. Brace expansion allows you to create multiple command line arguments from a single argument. The single argument is combined with all the strings that are given within the braces and creates as many new arguments as brace strings. Values in the braces can either be comma separated strings or a sequence expression. Examples of sequence expressions include {1..5} and {a..z}.

```
$ sudo cp /etc/passwd{,.bak}
$ ls /etc/passwd*
/etc/passwd  /etc/passwd.bak
$ mkdir -p ~/my-app/{bin,lib,log}
$ ls ~/my-app/
bin  lib  log
$ echo 10.0.0.{0..7}
10.0.0.0 10.0.0.1 10.0.0.2 10.0.0.3 10.0.0.4 10.0.0.5
```

```
10.0.0.6 10.0.0.7
```

Quickly Change a File's Extension

```
$ mv file{.old,.new}
```

To rename a file with a new extension employ brace expansion. This example changes a ".txt" file to a ".doc" file.

```
$ ls report*
report.txt
$ mv report.{txt,doc}
$ ls report*
report.doc
$
```

Here's another example.

```
$ ls httpd*
httpd.cfg
$ mv httpd.{cfg,conf}
$ ls httpd*
httpd.conf
$
```

This command will add an extension to a file.

```
$ ls jazz*
jazz
```

```
$ mv jazz{,.mp3}
$ ls jazz*
jazz.mp3
$
```

Create Backups of Files by Date with Ease

```
$ alias d='date +%F'
```

By using the date format of YYYY-MM-DD for file or directory names, you make ls output more human friendly. You can quickly tell the date order of the files when using this format.

```
$ ls -1 file*
file.2013-04-08
file.2013-12-21
file.2014-04-08
$ ls -1 other-file.*
other-file.04-08-2013
other-file.04-08-2014
other-file.12-21-2013
```

Before making a change to a file I like to make a backup copy of it. I also like to know when I made the backup. By creating an alias of "d" which is short for the date in YYYY-MM-DD format, I can quickly create these types of backups.

```
$ echo "alias d='date +%F'" >> ~/.bash_profile
$ ~/.bash_profile
$ d
```

```
2014-04-08
$ sudo cp httpd.conf httpd.conf.`d`
$ sudo cp httpd.conf httpd.conf.$(d)
$ sudo cp httpd.conf !#.$(d)
$ sudo cp httpd.conf{,.$(d)}
$ ls -1 httpd.conf*
httpd.conf
httpd.conf.2014-04-08
```

Overwrite the Contents of a File

```
$ command > file
```

You can redirect output from one command to a file using the greater-than symbol. A single greater-than symbol (>) redirects standard output to a file, overwriting (truncating) any existing contents of the file. If no file exists, it creates one.

```
$ grep bash /etc/passwd > users-that-use-bash
$ cat users-that-use-bash
root:x:0:0:root:/root:/bin/bash
jason:x:501:501:Jason:/home/jason:/bin/bash
oracle:x:1006:1006::/home/oracle:/bin/bash
bob:x:1000:1000:Bob Smith:/home/bob:/bin/bash
$
```

Empty a File That Is Being Written To

```
$ > file
$ cat /dev/null > file
```

To quickly zero out a file you can redirect nothing to it. Why not just delete the file and recreate it? If a process has a file open when you delete it, the process will keep the file handle open and continue writing to that file. Only when the process closes the file handle will the disk space used by that file be freed. If an application fills up /var and you delete the open log file, /var will still be full. If you redirect nothing to the file, the file is truncated and the application can continue writing to the file.

```
$ sudo -s
# > /var/log/maillog
# ls -l maillog
-rw-------. 1 root root 0 Apr  9 18:55 maillog
```

Append a String to a File

```
$ command >> file
```

The double greater than sign (>>) redirects standard output to a file and appends to any existing contents. If no file exists, it creates one.

```
$ echo build new server >> todo.txt
$ cat todo.txt
build new server
$ echo add server to the load balancer >> todo.txt
$ cat todo.txt
build new server
add server to the load balancer
$
```

Follow a File as It Grows

```
$ tail -f file
```

For a file that is constantly being update like a log file, use tail -f to view the updates to the file in real time.

```
$ tail -f /var/log/syslog
Apr 10 21:45:01 linww1 CRON[31769]: (root) CMD
(command -v debian-sa1 > /dev/null && debian-sa1 1 1)

Apr 10 21:46:28 linww1 whoopsie[1421]: online

Apr 10 21:47:37  whoopsie[1421]: last message
repeated 2 times

Apr 10 21:55:01 linww1 CRON[32548]: (root) CMD
(command -v debian-sa1 > /dev/null && debian-sa1 1 1)

Apr 10 22:05:01 linww1 CRON[931]: (root) CMD
(command -v debian-sa1 > /dev/null && debian-sa1 1 1)

Apr 10 22:15:01 linww1 CRON[2459]: (root) CMD
(command -v debian-sa1 > /dev/null && debian-sa1 1 1)

Apr 10 22:17:01 linww1 CRON[2609]: (root) CMD (    cd
/ && run-parts --report /etc/cron.hourly)

Apr 10 22:25:01 linww1 CRON[3197]: (root) CMD
(command -v debian-sa1 > /dev/null && debian-sa1 1 1)

Apr 10 22:35:01 linww1 CRON[4036]: (root) CMD
(command -v debian-sa1 > /dev/null && debian-sa1 1 1)

Apr 10 22:35:33 linww1 whoopsie[1421]: online
```

Watch Multiple Log Files at the Same Time

```
$ multitail file1 fileN
$ multitail file1 -I fileN
```

The multitail command allows you to browse through several files at once. Not only does multitail allow you to watch multiple files, it supports color highlighting, filtering, merging, and more. Here is a quick rundown of some of the most helpfuls commands for multitail.

F1 - Help
a - Add another file to follow
d - Delete a file from the view
/ - Start a search (Find)
ctrl-g - Exit a command, menu, or action. Similar to the emacs ctrl-g key binding.
q - Quit

```
$ sudo multitail /var/log/syslog  /var/log/kern.log

Apr 19 12:43:29 linuxsvr NetworkManager[758]: <info>
(eth0): IP6 addrconf timed out or failed.

Apr 19 12:43:29 linuxsvr NetworkManager[758]: <info>
Activation (eth0) Stage 4 of 5 (IPv6 Configure
Timeout) scheduled...

Apr 19 12:43:29 linuxsvr NetworkManager[758]: <info>
Activation (eth0) Stage 4 of 5 (IPv6 Configure
Timeout) started...

Apr 19 12:43:29 linuxsvr NetworkManager[758]: <info>
Activation (eth0) Stage 4 of 5 (IPv6 Configure
Timeout) complete.

00] /var/log/syslog *Press F1/<CTRL>+<h> for help*
132KB - 2014/04/19 12:46:45

Apr 19 12:43:08 linuxsvr kernel: [   10.012891]
Console: switching to colour frame buffer device
240x67

Apr 19 12:43:08 linuxsvr kernel: [   10.012926] fb0:
VESA VGA frame buffer device

Apr 19 12:43:11 linuxsvr kernel: [   12.288420] hda-
intel: Invalid position buffer, using LPIB read
```

method instead.

Apr 19 12:43:17 linuxsvr kernel: [18.891011] hda-
intel: IRQ timing workaround is activated for card
#0. Suggest a bigger bdl_pos_adj.

01] /var/log/kern.log *Press F1/<CTRL>+<h> for help*
132KB - 2014/04/19 12:46:45

To merge multiple files into one window, use the "-I" option. This intermixes the output of both of the files. This can aid in troubleshooting a problem.

```
$ sudo multitail /var/log/syslog -I /var/log/kern.log
```

Apr 19 12:43:08 linuxsvr kernel: [10.012891]
Console: switching to colour frame buffer device
240x67

Apr 19 12:43:08 linuxsvr kernel: [10.012926] fb0:
VESA VGA frame buffer device

Apr 19 12:43:11 linuxsvr kernel: [12.288420] hda-
intel: Invalid position buffer, using LPIB read
method instead.

Apr 19 12:43:17 linuxsvr kernel: [18.891011] hda-
intel: IRQ timing workaround is activated for card
#0. Suggest a bigger bdl_pos_adj.

Apr 19 12:43:29 linuxsvr NetworkManager[758]: <info>
Activation (eth0) Stage 4 of 5 (IPv6 Configure
Timeout) complete.

Apr 19 12:43:29 linuxsvr NetworkManager[758]: <info>
Activation (eth0) Stage 4 of 5 (IPv6 Configure
Timeout) scheduled...

Apr 19 12:43:29 linuxsvr NetworkManager[758]: <info>
Activation (eth0) Stage 4 of 5 (IPv6 Configure
Timeout) started...

Apr 19 12:43:29 linuxsvr NetworkManager[758]: <info>
(eth0): IP6 addrconf timed out or failed.

```
00] /var/log/syslog *Press F1/<CTRL>+<h> for help*
132KB - 2014/04/19 12:48:32
```

Delete Empty Directories

```
$ find . -type d -empty -delete
```

If you ever find yourself needing to clean up empty directories, find can make that task a snap. Use the -type d option to find all the directories with the -empty option to only include empty directories and finally the -delete option removes the directories.

```
$ mkdir -p testing/{1..4}
$ ls testing/
1  2  3  4
$ find . -type d -empty -delete
$ ls testing/
ls: cannot access testing/: No such file or directory
$
```

Print a List of Files That Contain a given String

```
$ grep -rl string .
```

To get a list of files that contain a given string, use grep with the -r (recursive) and -l (list files that match) options.

```
$ sudo grep -lr jim /var/log
/var/log/audit/audit.log.1
/var/log/secure-20140406
/var/log/secure
```

An Easy-to-Read Recursive File Listing

```
$ find . -type f -ls
```

The ls command has a recursive option, but I find reading the output from the find command to be easier to digest, especially for a large number of files and directories. The advantage to using find is that it displays the full path to each file, unlike ls.

```
$ ls -lR Music/
Music/:
total 4
drwxr-xr-x. 2 jason jason 4096 Feb 22 12:40 jazz
Music/jazz:
total 20932
-rw-r--r--. 1 jason jason       79496 Feb 22 12:40
giant-steps.mp3
-rw-r--r--. 1 jason jason 21267371 Feb 16 11:12 jazz-
album-1.mp3
-rw-r--r--. 1 jason jason       79496 Feb  3 18:13
john-coletrane.mp3
$ find Music/ -type f -ls
397966 20772 -rw-r--r--  1 jason jason 21267371 Feb
16 11:12 Music/jazz/jazz-album-1.mp3
396787    80 -rw-r--r--  1 jason jason  79496 Feb 22
12:40 Music/jazz/giant-steps.mp3
132464    80 -rw-r--r--  1 jason jason  79496 Feb  3
18:13 Music/jazz/john-coletrane.mp3
$
```

View Files and Directories in a Tree Format

```
$ tree
$ tree -d
$ tree -L number
```

The tree command displays files and directories in a tree like format. If you only want to see the directory structure, use the -d option. To limit the depth of the tree, use the -L option followed by a number.

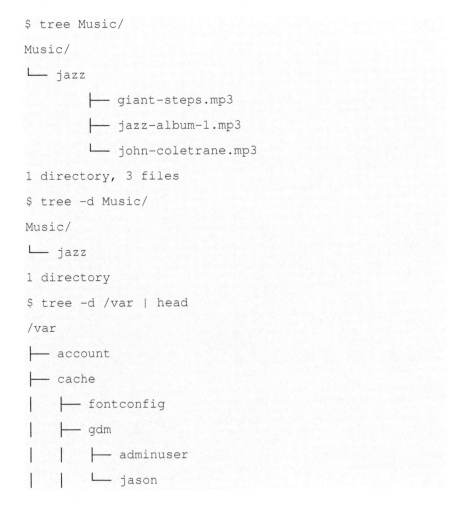

```
$ tree Music/
Music/
└── jazz
        ├── giant-steps.mp3
        ├── jazz-album-1.mp3
        └── john-coletrane.mp3
1 directory, 3 files
$ tree -d Music/
Music/
└── jazz
1 directory
$ tree -d /var | head
/var
├── account
├── cache
│   ├── fontconfig
│   ├── gdm
│   │   ├── adminuser
│   │   └── jason
```

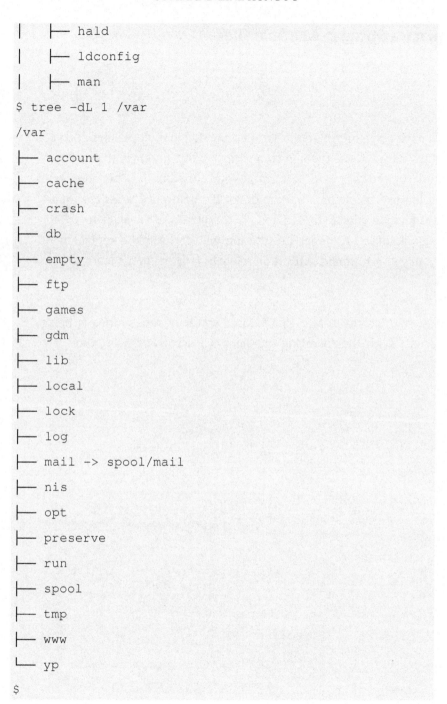

```
|      ├── hald
|      ├── ldconfig
|      ├── man
$ tree -dL 1 /var
/var
├── account
├── cache
├── crash
├── db
├── empty
├── ftp
├── games
├── gdm
├── lib
├── local
├── lock
├── log
├── mail -> spool/mail
├── nis
├── opt
├── preserve
├── run
├── spool
├── tmp
├── www
└── yp
$
```

Replace a String in Multiple Files

```
$ find /path -type f -exec sed -i.bak
's/string/replacement/g' {} \;
```

If you have some information that is embedded in multiple files and you need to change it, use the find command in combination with sed. The -i option for sed tells it to perform an in-place edit. You can supply an extension to -i to create a backup of the file before the edits are made. The command passed to sed tells it to substitute "replacement" for "string" globally. A global substitution will perform the replacement everywhere. A normal substitution replaces only the first occurrence on a line.

In this example the server that houses software repositories is being replaced. With the following one-liner, all occurrences of "thor" are replaced by "loki."

```
$ grep -r thor .
./deploy-il.sh:REPO_SERVER="thor.company.com"
./deploy-ca.sh:REPO_SERVER="thor.company.com"
./deploy-fl.sh:REPO_SERVER="thor.company.com"
./deploy-ny.sh:REPO_SERVER="thor.company.com"

$ find . -type f -exec sed -i.bak 's/thor/loki/g' {} \;
$ grep -r thor .
./deploy-fl.sh.bak:REPO_SERVER="thor.company.com"
./deploy-il.sh.bak:REPO_SERVER="thor.company.com"
./deploy-ny.sh.bak:REPO_SERVER="thor.company.com"
./deploy-ca.sh.bak:REPO_SERVER="thor.company.com"
```

```
$ grep -r loki .
./deploy-il.sh:REPO_SERVER="loki.company.com"
./deploy-ca.sh:REPO_SERVER="loki.company.com"
./deploy-fl.sh:REPO_SERVER="loki.company.com"
./deploy-ny.sh:REPO_SERVER="loki.company.com"
$
```

Extract the Nth Line from a File

```
$ awk 'NR==N'
```

To extract a specific line from a file, tell awk to print the line that matches the line number. One area where this comes in helpful is when you encounter an error in a script. To see exactly what the script is doing on that line, use awk.

```
$ ./deploy.sh
./deploy.sh: line 74: /usr/local/bin/patch: No such
file or directory
$ awk 'NR==74' deploy.sh
/usr/local/bin/patch $NEW_HOST
$
```

Convert Text Files from Windows Format to Linux Format and Vice-Versa

```
$ dos2unix
$ unix2dos
```

Sooner or later you're going to be sent a file or download one that uses a pair of CR (carriage return) and LF (line feed) characters to terminate lines in the file. Those type of files are Windows/DOS formatted. Unix-like operating systems simply use the LF character to terminate a line. Sometimes this can cause issues. To convert the file to a unix-like format, use dos2unix. To examine the line termination characters use "cat -A" or the "file" command.

```
$ cat -A from-my-windows-buddy.pl

#!/usr/bin/perl^M$

print "This is a cross-platform perl script!\n"^M$

$ ./from-my-windows-buddy.pl

-bash: ./from-my-windows-buddy.pl: /usr/bin/perl^M:
bad interpreter: No such file or directory

$ dos2unix from-my-windows-buddy.pl

dos2unix: converting file from-my-windows-buddy.pl to
UNIX format ...

$ cat -A from-my-windows-buddy.pl

#!/usr/bin/perl$

print "This is a cross-platform perl script!\n"$

$ ./from-my-windows-buddy.pl

This is a cross-platform perl script!

$ file other-file.txt

other-file.txt: ASCII text, with CRLF line
terminators

$ dos2unix other-file.txt

dos2unix: converting file other-file.txt to UNIX
format ...

$ file other-file.txt

other-file.txt: ASCII text

$
```

The opposite side of this coin is that if you send a file created on a Linux host to someone who opens it in Notepad on Windows, they will see just one long line of text. Convert the file to Windows/DOS format with the unix2dos command.

```
$ file report-for-ceo.txt
report-for-ceo.txt: ASCII text
$ unix2dos report-for-ceo.txt
unix2dos: converting file report-for-ceo.txt to DOS
format ...
$ file report-for-ceo.txt
report-for-ceo.txt: ASCII text, with CRLF line
terminators
$
```

MISCELLANEOUS

Change to the Previous Working Directory

```
$ cd -
```

If you want to return your previous working directory, use "cd -". The OLDPWD environment variable holds the path of your most recent directory location. "cd -" is the same as "cd $OLDPWD".

```
$ cd /etc/httpd/conf.d
$ grep ^SSLCert ssl.conf
SSLCertificateFile /etc/pki/tls/certs/localhost.crt
SSLCertificateKeyFile
/etc/pki/tls/private/localhost.key
$ cd /etc/pki/tls/certs/
$ ls
ca-bundle.crt  ca-bundle.trust.crt  localhost.crt
make-dummy-cert  Makefile  renew-dummy-cert
$ cd -
/etc/httpd/conf.d
```

```
$
```

Reset Your Terminal Emulator Display

```
$ reset
```

Displaying binary files to your screen can cause your terminal to become unusable. To attempt to recover, type "reset" and press enter. Your terminal may be in such a state that you won't be able to see what you're typing, but you shell will still accept the input.

```
$ cat blue-train.mp3
F□□□A□□□□□□h□reset
$
```

Search Wikipedia from the Command Line

```
$ dig +short txt <string>.wp.dg.cx
$ host -t txt <string>.wp.dg.cx
```

If you need to quickly look up some information on a subject, you can search wikipedia using DNS. The name server returns wikipedia article summaries as TXT records.

```
$ dig +short txt linux.wp.dg.cx
"Linux is a Unix-like computer operating system
assembled under the model of free and open source
software development and distribution. The defining
component of Linux is the Linux kernel, an operating
system kernel first released 5 October 1991 by Linus
Torvalds. http://en.wikipedia.org/wiki/Linux"
$ host -t txt bash_shell.wp.dg.cx
bash_shell.wp.dg.cx descriptive text "Bash is a Unix
```

shell written by Brian Fox for the GNU Project as a
free software replacement for the Bourne shell
(sh).Bash is a command processor, typically run in a
text window, allowing the user to type commands which
cause actions. Bash can also read commands from a
file, called a script. Like all Unix shells, it
supports filename wildcarding, piping, here
documents...
http://en.wikipedia.org/wiki/Bash_(Unix_shell)"

You can create a small shell script to save yourself from typing the full
DNS query each time.

```
$ echo -e '#!/bin/bash\ndig +short txt ${1}.wp.dg.cx'
> wikidig

$ chmod 755 !$

chmod 755 wikidig

$ ./wikidig ubuntu_operating_system
```

"Ubuntu As of 2012, according to online surveys,
Ubuntu is the most popular Linux distribution on
desktop/laptop personal computers, and most Ubuntu
coverage focuses on its use in that market. However,
it is also popular on servers and for cloud
computing.
http://en.wikipedia.org/wiki/Ubuntu_(operating_system
)"

Alternatively, you could create a function instead and add it to your dot
files.

```
$ echo 'wikidig() { dig +short txt ${1}.wp.dg.cx; }'
>> .bash_profile

$ . ~/.bash_profile
```

```
$ wikidig jazz

"Jazz is a musical style that originated at the
beginning of the 20th century in black communities in
the Southern United States. It was born out of a mix
of African and European music traditions. Its African
pedigree is evident in its use of blue notes,
improvisation, polyrhythms, syncopation and the swung
note. From its early development until the present
day jazz has also...
http://en.wikipedia.org/wiki/Jazz"
```

Make Non-Interactive Shell Sessions Behave the Same as Interactive Sessions

Make any customizations in ~/.bashrc. The contents of ~/.bash_profile:

```
if [ -f ~/.bashrc ]; then

source ~/.bashrc

fi
```

The shell behaves in slightly different ways when you log on interactively versus when you just connect to run a single command. The contents of .profile or .bash_profile are only executed for interactive sessions. If you are not aware of this subtle difference it may leave you scratching your head as to why something works perfectly when you log in and execute a command versus when you just ssh in to run that same command. You can save yourself some hassle by making your interactive and non-interactive sessions behave the same. To do this, configure .bash_profile to reference .bashrc and put all of your configuration in .bashrc.

Here is an example to better illustrate the difference between interactive and non-interactive shells. For example, if you define an alias for ll in ~/.bash_profile it will work during an interactive session but it will not be available during a non-interactive session.

Interactive:

```
mac:~ jason $ ssh linuxserver
jason@linuxserver:~$ uptime
 11:49:16 up 97 days,  2:59,  5 users,  load average:
0.15, 0.25, 0.31
jason@linuxserver:~$ ll
-rw-r--r-- 1 jason jason 221 Nov 13 11:30 file.txt
jason@linuxserver:~$ exit
logout
Connection to 10.0.1.9 closed.
mac:~ jason $
```

Non interactive:

```
mac:~ jason$ ssh linuxserver uptime
 11:49:16 up 97 days,  2:59,  5 users,  load average:
0.15, 0.25, 0.31
mac:~ jason$ ssh linuxserver ll
bash: ll: command not found
mac:~ jason$
```

```
$ cat .bash_profile
# Put our settings in .bashrc so we have the same
environment for login and non-login shells.
if [ -f ~/.bashrc ]; then
    source ~/.bashrc
```

```
fi
$ cat .bashrc
alias ll='ls -l'
HISTFILESIZE=5000
export HISTFILESIZE
```

Make Your Computer to Talk to You

```
$ espeak -f file
$ echo text | espeak
```

Espeak converts text to speech. You can provide espeak a file or pipe in text for it to speak. If you have a long running task you can let your computer tell you when it's finished as in this example.

```
$ for VIDEO in $(ls *.mp4 | sed 's/.mp4//')
> do
>   avconv -v quiet -i $x.mp4 $x.mp3
>done ; echo "File conversions complete." | espeak
```

Display the Current Date and Time
in a Different Time Zone

```
$ TZ=<TIMEZONE> date
```

The TZ environment variable specifies the time zone. If you want to know the time in a given time zone, prepend the environment variable and time zone to the date command.

```
$ TZ=America/Los_Angeles date
Sun Apr  6 19:37:46 PDT 2014
$ TZ=MST date
```

```
Sun Apr   6 19:37:48 MST 2014
$ TZ=CST date
Mon Apr   7 02:37:50 CST 2014
$ TZ=UTC date
Mon Apr   7 02:37:53 UTC 2014
```

It's a common practice to use UTC as the time zone on servers. If your workstation or laptop is set to a different time zone, you can create an alias that quickly gives you the time in UTC.

```
$ alias utc='TZ=UTC date'
$ utc
Mon Apr   7 02:35:01 UTC 2014
```

Display a Calendar at the Command Line

```
$ cal
$ cal MM YYYY
$ cal YYYY
```

To display an calendar at the command line use the cal command. Use the -3 option to display the previous, current, and next month. If you want to see the calendar for an specific month use MM YYYY or for an entire year use YYYY.

```
$ cal
        April 2014
Su Mo Tu We Th Fr Sa
        1  2  3  4  5
 6  7  8  9 10 11 12
13 14 15 16 17 18 19
20 21 22 23 24 25 26
27 28 29 30
$ cal -3
      March 2014              April 2014              May 2014
Su Mo Tu We Th Fr Sa    Su Mo Tu We Th Fr Sa    Su Mo Tu We Th Fr Sa
                  1           1  2  3  4  5                  1  2  3
 2  3  4  5  6  7  8     6  7  8  9 10 11 12     4  5  6  7  8  9 10
 9 10 11 12 13 14 15    13 14 15 16 17 18 19    11 12 13 14 15 16 17
16 17 18 19 20 21 22    20 21 22 23 24 25 26    18 19 20 21 22 23 24
23 24 25 26 27 28 29    27 28 29 30             25 26 27 28 29 30 31
30 31
$ 10 2014
        October 2014
Su Mo Tu We Th Fr Sa
           1  2  3  4
 5  6  7  8  9 10 11
12 13 14 15 16 17 18
19 20 21 22 23 24 25
26 27 28 29 30 31
```

Extract a Tar Archive to a Different Directory

```
$ tar tarfile.tar -C /path/to/directory
```

Instead of changing directories and untarring a file, you can use the -C option.

```
$ tar xf projectfiles.tar -C /usr/local/myproject
```

This is equivalent to these two commands.

```
$ cd /usr/local/myproject
$ tar xf ~/projectfiles.tar
```

Transform the Directory Structure
of a Tar File When Extracting It

```
$ tar xf tarfile.tar --strip-components=NUMBER
```

If you want to extract a tar file starting at a subdirectory, use the --strip-components option. For example, if you download a release from github.com the name and version of the project is the top directory in the tar file. To extract the files below that directory use --strip-components=1.

```
$ curl -sLO
https://github.com/twbs/bootstrap/archive/v3.1.1.tar.
gz
$ tar ztvf v3.1.1.tar.gz   | head -1
drwxrwxr-x root/root              0 2014-02-13 12:24
bootstrap-3.1.
$  tar zxvf v3.1.1.tar.gz  --strip-components=1 -C
~/bootstrap-latest
$ ls -1 ~/bootstrap-latest
bower.json
```

```
CNAME

composer.json

_config.yml

CONTRIBUTING.md

dist

docs

fonts

grunt

Gruntfile.js

js

less

LICENSE

package.json

README.md

test-infra
```

Use a Spreadsheet from the Command Line

```
$ sc
```

If you're the kind of person that tries to do absolutely everything at the command line, then you'll like the spreadsheet calculator, SC. Also, if you're comfortable with vi, then sc will come naturally to you. In addition to using the arrow keys for navigation you can use the familiar h, j, k, and l keys. Like vi, g represents go. To go the cell D4 type gD4.

To enter a number or a formula navigate to the cell you want to edit and use = followed by the number or formula. To enter left justified text use the less-than sign (<) and the greater-than sign (>) for right justified text. To edit a cell type e. To save a file, press P followed by a filename. For quick help type ? and to quit, type q. For more information check out the tutorial that ships with SC.

```
$ sc
A2 (10 2 0)  [@sum(A0:A1)]
                    A            B            C
   0              1.00
   1              3.00
   2              4.00
$ sc /usr/share/doc/sc/tutorial.sc
```

Rudimentary Command Line Stopwatch

```
$ time read
```

This command will stop when you press enter and display how much time elapsed. The real row contains the elapsed time.

```
$ time read
real     0m8.047s
user     0m0.000s
sys      0m0.000s
$
```

Repeat a Command at Regular Intervals and Watch Its Changing Output

```
$ watch command
```

If you want to monitor the output of a command, use watch. Watch will execute a command periodically and display its output. You can control the interval that the command is repeated by supplying a number of seconds to the -n option. This is great tool to watch processes, disk usage, number of logged in users, queue depths, etc.

```
$ sudo /usr/local/bin/compress-log-files &
[1] 15650
$ watch df -h /var
Filesystem                         Size   Used Avail
Use% Mounted on
/dev/mapper/vg_livecd-lv_root    28G   3.7G    24G   14%
/

...

Filesystem                         Size   Used Avail
Use% Mounted on
/dev/mapper/vg_livecd-lv_root    28G   3.3G    25G   12%
/
$ watch -n 1 "ps -ef| grep httpd | grep -v grep | wc
-l"
9

...

14

...

29

...

27

$
```

Execute a Command at a given Time

```
$ echo "command" | at time
$ at -f file time
```

If you ever need to reboot a server at midnight, but don't feel like staying up that late, schedule it with the at command. Actually you can schedule any command or set of commands that you need to run once at a given time with at. To list your at jobs use atq. Here's the reboot example.

```
$ sudo -s
# echo 'reboot' | at midnight
# atq
1     2014-04-13 00:00 a root
# exit
$ exit
```

You can provide at with a series of commands in a file by using the -f option. For example, you could send your boss a report at 5:00 PM on Friday and leave early to play a round of golf. If your conscience gets the better of you, you can delete your at job with atrm.

```
$ at -f email-tps-report-to-boss 5:00pm friday
job 2 at 2014-04-18 17:00
$ atrm 2
$ atq
$
```

Share Your Screen Session with Another User

```
$ screen -x user/session
```

In order to use multi user support for screen, the screen executable needs to be setuid for root.

```
$ sudo chmod u+s /usr/bin/screen
```

One user must start a screen session. It can be helpful to name your screen sessions with the -S option. To enable multi user session, type ctrl-a followed by ":multiuser on<enter>". To allow someone to connect to your session type ctrl-a followed by ":acladd username". To disconnect the other user from the screen session type ctrl-a followed by ":acldel username".

```
[jason@linuxsvr ~]$ screen -S for-bob
ctrl-a :multiuser on
Multiuser mode enabled
ctrl-a :acladd bob
```

When the other use is ready to connect to the screen session, they type screen -x followed by the session identifier. They can connect by PID or by name. IE, screen -x 1234 or screen -x session-name. When they are ready to disconnect, they can leave the screen session like any other by typing ctrl-a d. While the session is shared both parties not only can they see the same screen, but they both provide input by typing.

```
bob@linuxsvr:~$ screen -ls jason/
There is a suitable screen on:
        5428.for-bob        (Multi, attached)
1 Socket in /var/run/screen/S-jason.
bob@linuxsvr:~$ screen -x jason/for-bob
```

```
[jason@linuxsvr ~]$
ctrl-a d
[detached]
bob@linuxsvr:~$
```

Execute an Unaliased Version of an Aliased Command

```
$ \aliased-command
```

Use the escape character to ignore an alias for a command. For example, if "ls" is aliased to "ls -F", use "\ls" to execute "ls" without the "-F" option. The "-F" option to ls appends a file type indicator. In the case of directories that indicator is a forward slash (/).

```
$ alias ls
alias ls='ls -F'
$ ls
Desktop/  Documents/  Downloads/  examples.desktop
$ \ls
Desktop  Documents  Downloads  examples.desktop
$
```

Save the Output of a Command as an Image

```
$ command | convert label:@- image.png
```

To capture the output of a command in an image file, use the convert command from the ImageMagick software suite. If you want to email a password to someone, but don't want it travel around the Internet in plain text, put it in an image. When supplying the at sign (@) to label it tells convert to read input from the file following the at sign. The dash says the "file" is coming from standard input. If you want to create a simple image with some text you can supply a string to label.

```
$ echo "bob:changeme" | sudo chpasswd
$ echo "bob:changeme" | convert label:@- password.png
$ convert label:"bob:changeme" same-thing-different-
way.png
$ echo "Here's your password.  Again." | mail -a
passwd.png -s 'Password reset' bob@mycompany.com
$
```

ABOUT THE AUTHOR

Jason Cannon started his career as a Unix and Linux System Engineer in 1999. Since that time he has utilized his Linux skills at companies such as Xerox, UPS, Hewlett-Packard, and Amazon.com. Additionally, he has acted as a technical consultant and independent contractor for small to medium businesses.

Jason has professional experience with CentOS, RedHat Enterprise Linux, SUSE Linux Enterprise Server, and Ubuntu. He has used several Linux distributions on personal projects including Debian, Slackware, CrunchBang, and others. In addition to Linux, Jason has experience supporting proprietary Unix operating systems including AIX, HP-UX, and Solaris.

He enjoys teaching others how to use and exploit the power of the Linux operating system and teaches online video training courses at http://www.LinuxTrainingAcademy.com.

Jason is also the author of *Linux for Beginners: An Introduction to the Linux Operating System and Command Line.*

OTHER BOOKS BY THE AUTHOR

High Availability for the LAMP Stack: Eliminate Single Points of Failure and Increase Uptime for Your Linux, Apache, MySQL, and PHP Based Web Applications
http://www.linuxtrainingacademy.com/ha-lamp-book

Linux for Beginners: An Introduction to the Linux Operating System and Command Line
http://www.linuxtrainingacademy.com/linux

The Linux Screenshot Tour Book: An Illustrated Guide to the Most Popular Linux
Distributions
http://www.linuxtrainingacademy.com/screenshots

Python Programming for Beginners: An Introduction to the Python Computer Language and Computer Programming
http://www.linuxtrainingacademy.com/python-book

COURSES BY THE AUTHOR

High Availability for the LAMP Stack
http://www.linuxtrainingacademy.com/ha-lamp-stack/

Linux for Beginners
http://www.linuxtrainingacademy.com/lfb-udemy

Learn Linux in 5 Days
http://www.linuxtrainingacademy.com/linux-in-5-days

INDEX

APPENDIX

Trademarks

Firefox is a registered trademark of the Mozilla Foundation.

ImageMagick is a registered trademark of ImageMagick Studio LLC.

Linux® is the registered trademark of Linus Torvalds in the U.S. and other countries.

Mac and OS X are trademarks of Apple Inc., registered in the U.S. and other countries.

Open Source is a registered certification mark of Open Source Initiative.

Sun and Oracle Solaris are trademarks or registered trademarks of Oracle Corporatoin and/or its affiliates in the United States and other countries.

UNIX is a registered trademark of The Open Group.

Windows is a registered trademark of Microsoft Corporation in the United States and other countries.

All other product names mentioned herein are the trademarks of their respective owners.

Printed in Great Britain
by Amazon

15414865R00071